Deserts Activity Book

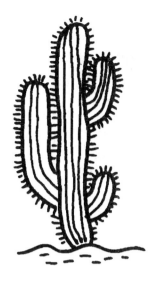

Author	Ellen Sussman
Editor	Kathy Rogers
Illustrator	Barb Lorseyedi
Page Design	Linda Milliken
Cover Design	Imaginings

METRIC CONVERSION CHART

Refer to this chart when metric conversions are not found within the activity.

¼ tsp	=	1 ml	350° F	=	180° C
½ tsp	=	2 ml	375° F	=	190° C
1 tsp	=	5 ml	400° F	=	200° C
1 Tbsp	=	15 ml	425° F	=	216° C
¼ cup	=	60 ml	1 inch	=	2.54 cm
⅓ cup	=	80 ml	1 foot	=	30 cm
½ cup	=	125 ml	1 yard	=	91 cm
1 cup	=	250 ml	1 mile	=	1.6 km
1 oz.	=	28 g			
1 lb.	=	.45 kg			

EP118 • ©1998, 2002 Edupress, Inc.™ • P.O. Box 883 • Dana Point, CA 92629
www.edupressinc.com
ISBN 1-56472-118-3
Printed in USA

Table of Contents

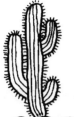

Literature List

• **Life in the Desert**
by Andrew Clements;
Steck-Vaughn 1998. (2-4)
Spectacular photographs depict the beauty
and diversity of the world's deserts, their
land formations, and the plant and animal
life they support. Practical suggestions
prepare readers for their first desert visit.

• **Deserts**
by Seymour Simon;
Mulberry Books 1990. (2-4)
Photographs and clearly-written text
describe the nature and characteristics of
deserts, where they are located, and how
they are formed.

• **All About Deserts**
by John Sanders;
Troll Associates 1984. (2-5)
Uses a question-and-answer format to
present basic information about deserts.
Appealing and colorful illustrations.

• **Desert Giant**
by Barbara Bash;
Sierra Club Books 1989. (3-6)
Documents the life cycle and ecosystem of
the giant saguaro cactus and the desert
animals it helps to support. The lovely
watercolor artwork supports the text in a
warm and tender way.

• **Storm on the Desert**
by Carolyn Lesser;
Harcourt Brace & Co. 1997. (1-4)
Describes the animal and plant life in a
desert in the American southwest and the
effects of a short but violent thunderstorm.
Brilliant and colorful pastel, pencil, chalk,
and watercolor artwork on every page.

• **Deserts**
by Angela Wilkes;
Hayes Books 1980. (3-6)
A fact-filled guide to desert life; each
caption is illustrated and very clearly
explained.

• **Expanding Deserts**
by Paula Hogan;
Gareth Stevens 1991. (3-6)
Discusses the causes of desertification and
what can be done to stop the spread of
deserts.

• **The Desert Is Theirs**
by Byrd Baylor;
Aladdin 1975. (2-5)
A soft and gentle story with simple text
and illustrations that describe the
characteristics of the desert and its plant,
animal, and human life.

• **Sand on the Move**
by Roy A. Gallant;
Franklin Watts 1997. (4-6)
Discusses the different types of sand
dunes, how they form and move, the
destruction they can cause, and the animal
and plant life they support.

• **Cactus Hotel**
by Brenda Z. Guiberson;
Henry Holt & Co. 1991. (1-4)
Describes the life cycle of the giant
saguaro cactus with an emphasis on its role
as a home for other desert dwellers.

• **Out to Dry**
by June Swanson;
Lerner Publications Co. 1994. (2-6)
Clever and funny riddles about the desert.

Glossary

arroyo—a cut in the land made by rushing rain water.

burrow—a hole in the ground dug by nocturnal desert animals as a shelter from the desert sun.

butte—land that juts out due to wind blowing and cutting it over a long period of time.

cactus—spiny, prickly, mostly leafless plants able to store water and survive desert climates; they often have showy flowers.

canyon—a large cut in the land made by a river.

caravan—a long train of people and pack animals such as camels, mules, and llamas that travel through barren country.

desert—a large area of dry land that receives less than ten inches (25.4 cm) of rain annually; a region that can support little vegetation because of both insufficient rainfall and dry soil.

desertification—a process by which land becomes unable to support plant or animal life.

drought—a period when much less rain falls than is normal, causing extreme dryness.

dunes—mounds of sand created and shaped by the wind.

erosion—the wearing away of land and rock by wind, water, rain, and other forces.

gemsbok—an antelope with black and white streaks and long sharp horns that inhabits the Kalahari Desert in southern Africa.

Gila monster—a poisonous lizard that inhabits some deserts.

irrigate—to supply the land with water using pipes and ditches.

mesa—broad, flat-topped mountain with sharp, rocky slopes.

mesquite—a small desert tree with deep roots.

mirage—a trick of the light; hot air above the ground acts like a mirror and reflects the sky, making it look like a sheet of water on the ground.

nomads—people who move from one place to another as a way of making a living; desert nomads move mainly in search of water and grazing land.

North American deserts—deserts located in the southwestern part of the U.S. and the northern part of Mexico.

oasis—a fertile place in a desert, due to the presence of water.

saguaro cactus—the largest cactus plant that can grow up to 50 feet (15.24 m) and grows in the Sonoran desert in the western U.S.

Sahara—the world's largest desert, located in northern Africa.

sandstorm—a high wind in which sand is carried and blown about.

sidewinder—a poisonous rattlesnake that moves through the desert in a series of curves.

tarantula—a very large and hairy desert spider.

topsoil—the fertile layer of soil on the surface of the ground.

valleys—low land between hills or mountains.

wasteland—barren, dry land that cannot support any life.

The World's Deserts

Information

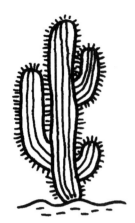

To most people, a desert is a waterless, very hot, windy place with few signs of life. Some deserts are just like that; others are quite different. There are deserts that get no rain at all and others where it may rain ten times a year. Some deserts have scrubby bushes and others are filled with cactus. Some deserts are covered with tall towers of oddly-shaped rocks while others are covered with salty lakes and flats.

A particular combination of rainfall, temperature, location, and landscape define a desert. While each desert is distinct, they are also alike in certain ways and all of them have one thing in common—they are all dry. Any place where the rainfall (or snowfall) is less than ten inches (25.4 cm) a year is a desert.

Most deserts can be found north and south of the equator in two narrow belts that circle the Earth.

Project

Locate the major deserts of the world and write a weather description for each desert.

Materials

- World Deserts map pages, following
- Transparency film
- Overhead projector
- Resource books
- Paper
- Pencil

Directions

1. Duplicate the map pages. Enlarge the patterns and transfer to transparency film.

2. Working with the overhead projector, point to and call out the following map locations and deserts. Have children locate each callout on their map and label their copy.
   - Label the *equator*, the *Tropic of Cancer*, the *Tropic of Capricorn*.
   - Find *Africa*. Label the *Sahara* and the *Kalahari Deserts*.
   - Find *Asia*. Label the *Turkestan, Indian, Arabian*, and *Gobi Deserts*.
   - Find *Australia*. Label the *Australian Desert*.
   - Find *South America*. Label the *Atacama* and the *Patagonian Deserts*.
   - Find *North America*. Label the *Great Basin*, the *Mojave, Sonoran*, and *Chihuahuan Deserts*.

3. Divide the class into small groups. Assign one desert to each group. Research the special weather conditions that affect their assigned desert and present their findings to the class.

The World's Deserts

The World's Deserts

Desert Landscape

Information

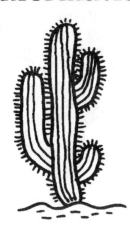

The wind does some unusual things in the desert. It causes spiraling columns of dust to shoot up into the air. It blows the sand so that it moves and changes direction and makes it appear like ripples of water. Wind-blown sand hits against rocks and changes their appearance over long periods of time. And moving sand can pile up to make large sand dunes.

Wind, along with sudden rain and heat, make pieces of many rocks break off. Areas that were once almost entirely flat can change into areas of massive jagged rock. Due to continual natural, weather, and climatic conditions, the desert landscape includes various land formations such as *arroyos*, *buttes*, *mesas*, and canyons created by erosion.

Project

Create three-dimensional exhibits of desert landscape features.

Directions

1. Make one copy of the Desert Dictionary cards on the following page.

2. Divide the class into nine groups. Assign each group one card. Each group is responsible for researching the word on their card, and working cooperatively to create a three-dimensional exhibit or diorama illustrating the definition of the desert landscape word. Set a completion date for the project.

3. Display final dioramas with the Desert Dictionary card attached.

Materials

- Desert Dictionary cards, following
- Sand, clay, water, paint, brushes, small cartons and shoe boxes, cardboard, construction paper, scissors, paste, other craft supplies as needed
- Resource books

Desert Dictionary Cards

Arroyo
The desert drainage system is made up of dried streams called arroyos. After a heavy rainfall, rushing water fills the arroyos. It runs down the mountains making big cuts or gullies in the land, carrying deposits of gravel, rock, and sand to the bottom.

Canyon
Over time, an arroyo can become a canyon. Canyons are larger and deeper than arroyos and they are cut by streams and rivers. Rivers can cut very deep canyons. The famous Grand Canyon was cut by the Colorado River.

Butte
Strong winds in a desert pick up dry sand and soil and blow it at rocks and hills. Over a long period of time, the blowing sand can cut rock to look like a flat-topped tower called a butte.

Alluvial Fan
Deposits of sand, rock, and gravel carried by the rushing waters that form arroyos create fan-shaped forms that are called alluvial fans.

Playa
After a rainfall, mountain streams carry water and salt into playas—dry lake beds that have no outlet. The water that collects there either evaporates or seeps into the earth. The salt remains and builds up on the surface.

Dune
Parts of a desert may be covered by windswept piles of sand called dunes. They are made when sand piles up in mounds. Dunes may reach heights of 820 feet (250 m).

Mesa
Rainstorms and fierce winds help shape the way deserts look. High, broad, and flat-topped mountains with sharp, rocky slopes called mesas can rise hundreds of feet above the desert floor.

Oasis
Oases occur throughout a desert. Many of these fertile areas lie near springs or underground streams. An artificial oasis may also be created by surface irrigation.

Cactus
Cactus plants are green, fleshy, mostly leafless, spiny and prickly plants native to regions of North America. They can expand to store water after a rainstorm. Cacti often have showy flowers.

9

Desertification

Information

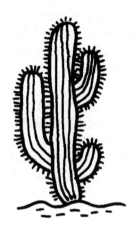

Desertification is the term scientists use for the process by which land becomes unable to support life. Deserts in many parts of the world are increasing in number and size. Long droughts are being endured in some areas. Because people misuse the farmlands at the edges of deserts, the land turns to bare and dry wasteland, unable to support any plant or animal life.

People who live on the edges of deserts grow crops in these farmland areas. They cut down trees for firewood. Their sheep, cows, and goats may eat so much grass that it is unable to grow back. Seeds are unable to sprout because heavy-footed animals have packed the soil down firmly with their hooves.

The forces of weather also play a part in desertification. Wind picks up fertile topsoil and blows it away. Soil once held in place by roots of plants is washed away by rain. This process of erosion changes the desert land forever. Lost topsoil cannot be replaced.

Project

Conduct an experiment to discover how desertification affects an area's capability to support plants.

Directions

1. Fill one container with potting soil; fill the other with sand.

2. Plant lettuce seeds in each container.

3. Place both containers on a sunny window ledge and water them lightly every three or four days.

4. Compare the plant growth after one, two, and three weeks.

5. What conclusions can you draw about the differences in growth?

Materials

• Two planting containers (the same size)
• Potting soil
• Sand
• Lettuce seeds

Desert Rainfall

Information

Although deserts get low amounts of rainfall, rainstorms help shape the way they look. Monument Valley on the Arizona-Utah border was formed by strong winds and sudden rainstorms over thousands of years. If this rainfall was spread out evenly during the year, rainwater would be able to sink slowly into the soil, allowing grass to grow.

But desert rains are short and violent. Water can't sink into lower ground layers. It collects on land surfaces and flows downhill, causing flash floods. As the water rushes down hillsides, it carries sand, rocks, and even boulders. A fast stream can cut into solid rock like a sandblaster. The surging rains cut deep channels leaving behind gullies or arroyos—dry beds of sand and rock. Most erosion happens during big floods when a landslide may bring down part of a mountain.

Many plants and animals only flower and reproduce after rain when their seeds and offspring have the best chance of survival.

Project

Create a clay model of a hilly terrain and simulate a rainfall.

Materials

- *Storm on the Desert* by Carolyn Lesser (see Literature List, page 3)
- Clay, soil, small rocks
- Watering can, water
- Kettle
- Two large trays with deep sides (an aluminum roasting pan works well)

Directions

1. Discuss your experiences with rain water. Where does rain water go?

2. In each tray, create a clay model of a hilly terrain, including valleys and depressions to simulate natural terrain. Place soil and rocks on each clay model. Use a watering can to simulate rain on one model. On the other model pour water from a large kettle.

3. Make observations about how the water affects the clay models. How are the results in the trays different? Draw conclusions about the effect of rainstorms on desert land.

4. Read *Storm on the Desert*—the description of a fierce summer storm in the American southwest and the animal and plant life affected by it.

Modern Irrigation

Information

In dry areas where water is scarce, farmers must *irrigate* their fields for the crops to survive. Older methods of irrigation have proven wasteful because too much water evaporated before it reached the crops.

Farmers are now using new irrigation methods to cut down on water waste. On large farms, pumps have built-in computers to draw water from underground. The computer can measure how dry the soil is and spray just the right amount of water on the crops. As less water is used, less is wasted. *Drip irrigation* reduces evaporation. A long hose with tiny holes is placed on the ground close to the plant's roots. Water slowly drips out of the hose. Almost all the water is absorbed by the roots of the plants and very little evaporates into the air. By placing heavy plastic sheets at the base of plants, the soil stays moist. The plastic also keeps water-drinking weeds from growing.

Project

Conduct experiments to learn about evaporation.

Materials

- Cloth cut into three equal-sized pieces
- Two saucers

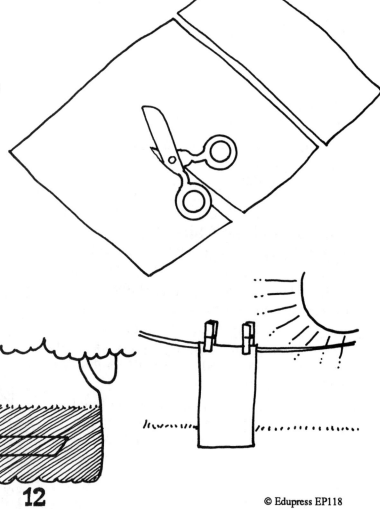

Directions

1. Cut a piece of wet cloth into three equal pieces. Lay one piece flat in the sun, lay one flat in the shade, and hang one in the sun. Observe to see which one dries the fastest.

2. Fill two saucer plates of the same size with water. Place one on a sunny window ledge; place the other one in the refrigerator. Observe and compare after two days. Which saucer had more evaporation?

3. Draw conclusions about the results of the two experiments and relate them to desert conditions.

Oases

Information

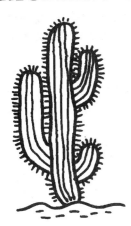

Oases are water spots in desert regions. Some oases are so small that they can only provide enough water for a few people. Other oases are so huge that they can support one million people. Egypt's Nile River flows along a 1,000-mile (1,600-km) stretch of the Sahara Desert, and the Colorado River crosses part of the North American Desert.

While the soil in deserts is generally fertile, it lacks enough moisture for plants to grow and thrive. Oases develop in places where springs, underground streams, or wells furnish water. Sometimes water can bubble up to the surface through a break in the rocks. Oases in the Sahara Desert result from springs and streams, or from close proximity to mountains which are high enough to cause moisture in the air to condense and produce rain.

In desert areas with no oases, some animals rarely drink. They get all the water they need from seeds and stems they eat. Snakes and lizards get their water from animals upon which they prey.

Project

- Conduct temperature tests to understand the differences between an oasis and the desert that surrounds it.
- Enjoy a rest on an oases with a refreshing desert salad.

Directions

1. Measure and record the temperature:
   - in a sunny spot with no trees
   - in a shady spot
   - near a pond or source of water
   - in the classroom

2. Compare the temperatures found in the different locations. What factors made the temperatures higher or lower. Relate your answers to weather conditions on an oasis.

3. Assign children to bring in various fruits. As part of this project, find out (from the manager of the produce section in the local market) where the fruit came from. Most packing cartons will indicate this.

4. Wash, cut, and mix fruit in a large bowl. Sprinkle lightly with sugar. Add lemon juice—another desert fruit—and serve.

Materials

- Indoor/outdoor thermometer
- Resource books
- Dates, apricots, cantaloupe, grapes, lemon juice, sugar
- Large mixing bowl
- Serving spoon and small paper bowls

Sand Dunes

Information

Sand dunes may be found in deserts and along the coasts of oceans, rivers, and lakes. They may vary in size from that of an anthill to a tall 15-story building. Every sand dune is a pile of sand built up by the wind. Once sand has been picked up by wind, it will go wherever the wind carries it. Eventually the wind drops the load of sand.

Some dunes are formed when the wind meets an object in its path. If the wind is blowing against a large rock or small bush, it may change direction and move around the object. As it hits the object, the wind drops many grains of sand in that spot. In a short time, a mound of wind-blown sand piles up in front of the object.

As more sand continues to be swept up the dune, the dune moves slowly in the direction of the wind. Over time, a dune changes in size, shape, and location. A dune can move 50 to 150 feet (15.24 to 45.72 meters) or more in a year depending on the wind force and the size of the sand particles in the dune.

Project

Investigate sand dunes.

Directions

1. Divide class into cooperative work groups. Assign each group one of these dune topics:
   - Singing or acoustic dunes
   - Dune areas in the U.S.
   - Types and shapes of dunes
   - Plant life in dunes
   - Animal life in dunes

2. Set a time for research and investigations to be completed.

3. In addition to reporting orally, each group reports their facts using three-dimensional models, charts, illustrations, photographs, or maps.

4. If a large area of sand is available, students reporting on acoustic dunes may want to form a miniature dune and try to stomp on it to see if they can hear any booming or vibrating sounds.

Materials

- Resource books
- Maps
- Large area of sand (optional)

From Rock to Sand

Information

Most of the sand you see today was once part of a rock. Although rocks may seem indestructible, they are subject to weathering. When rocks are exposed to rushing waters, crashing waves, heavy rains, and very strong winds over a long period they begin to crumble and erode. The intense heat of the daytime sun and the freezing cold of the night cause rocks to expand and contract. As they do, they break apart into smaller pieces.

When water flows into a rock's cracks and crevices—and then freezes—the rock may split into several pieces. Rocks also break up as they are forced to rub against each other.

The rocks of a desert are finally broken down into grains of sand. They become smaller and rounder as the wind bounces and rubs them one against another.

Project

- Conduct an experiment to discover what effects weather has on rocks.
- Make sand by rubbing rocks together.

Materials

- Modeling clay
- Plastic food wrap
- Water
- Freezer
- A variety of rocks

Directions

See what happens to a ball of clay as it warms and freezes.

1. Moisten a piece of modeling clay and roll it into two balls. Wrap each one in a piece of plastic food wrap.

2. Leave one in the classroom; put the other one in the freezer overnight.

3. Remove the clay from the freezer the following morning.

4. Unwrap both balls and compare them. Record your observations.

5. Put the ball of clay back into the freezer overnight. Are the cracks bigger the next day? What conclusions can you draw about the effects of cold temperatures on rocks and how they break down?

6. Experiment further with larger balls of clay to see if size affects the cracking.

7. Rub two rocks together onto a sheet of newsprint. Do the rocks break up into tiny particles? Do some rocks break up more easily than others?

PLASTIC WRAP

The Desert's Resources

Information

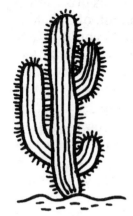

    While water may be the single most valuable part of the desert's resources, there are other valuable things to be found in the world's deserts. Vast amounts of oil and natural gas are found under the Sahara Desert. Precious metals like silver and gold have been mined from the North American deserts in the southwestern part of the U.S. Nitrates, which are excellent fertilizers, come from the Atacama Desert in South America. Valuable and highly sought-after minerals such an uranium, copper, diamonds, borax, gypsum, salt, and phosphates are found in many of the world's deserts.

Project

Create a tabletop exhibit of products containing resources found in the desert.

Materials

• Reference books

Directions

1. Use reference books to learn about the minerals listed above and how they are used. Also look for other kinds of resources provided by the desert.

2. Brainstorm a list of products that you might find at home or at the store that contain some of these resources.

3. Conduct a survey of your home and supermarket shelves, carefully reading labels to identify any of the listed materials. Bring items from home that are on the list.

4. Create a tabletop display of the products, labelling each product with the name of the desert resource it contains. Also include a written list of products you could not bring in as samples.

North American Deserts

Information

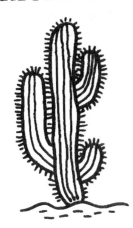

The deserts of North America cover wide areas of the southwestern United States and northern Mexico. The Great Basin Desert covers much of Nevada, Utah, Oregon, and Idaho, and spreads into Arizona, Colorado, Wyoming, and California. The eastern parts of the Sonoran Desert receive as much as ten inches (25.4 cm) of rain a year while the western parts are very dry. The Sonoran Desert is home to the best known desert plants—the cactus.

White Sands National Monument in New Mexico is part of the Chihuahuan Desert—the largest desert in North America. Most of this desert lies in Mexico. The yucca and the creosote bush are hardy enough to grow in this parched soil.

The Mojave Desert in California is home to Death Valley National Monument. Summer temperatures of 125°F (52°C) in the shade are common. Plants that can survive this heat include the creosote bush, desert holly, and mesquite.

Project

Experiment to see how desert plants get moisture from sand that appears dry.

Materials

- Shovel for digging
- Cup
- Sheet of plastic
- Several stones

Directions

1. Find a site in sandy soil for digging a hole and ask for permission to dig.

2. Dig a hole approximately two feet (61 cm) deep by 1½ feet (46 cm) wide.

3. Place a cup in the bottom center of the hole. Cover the hole with a piece of plastic sheet and place stones around the edges to secure it.

4. Place a large stone in the center of the sheet—over the cup to pull the sheet downward.

5. Observe as drops of water form on the underside of the plastic sheet and fall into the cup.

6. What conclusions can children draw about how this occurs?

(The sun warmed the exposed sand in the hole. Moisture held by the sand evaporated and condensed—or re-formed as water—on the plastic sheet.)

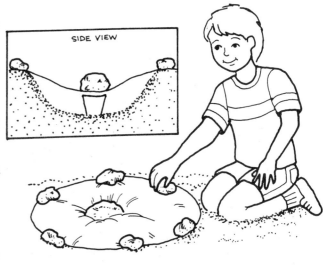

SIDE VIEW

Deserts Activity Book   © Edupress EP118

The Painted Desert

Information

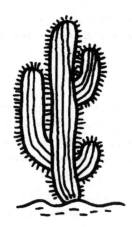

The Painted Desert is a brilliantly-colored region of plateaus extending about 200 miles (322 km) along the Little Colorado River in the north central part of Arizona. Early Spanish explorers named this region *El Desierto Pintado,* meaning the Painted Desert.

The pastel colors of the desert add to its natural beauty. The heat, light, and even the dust seem to change colors from blue, amethyst, and yellow to rust, lilac, and red. The desert is especially beautiful at sunrise and sunset when the colors are the most brilliant and the shadows are the deepest.

This vast area has buttes, mesas, pinnacles, and valleys formed by ages of wind and rain which cut into the volcanic ash. The bright reds and yellows come from the iron oxides in the rock of the region.

Project

Create a tissue-paper collage to reflect the colors of the Painted Desert.

Materials

- Tissue paper in colors mentioned above
- White glue, water, and containers
- Flat-tipped paint brushes
- Art paper
- Scissors (optional)
- Photographs of the Painted Desert
- Plastic sheet

Directions

1. Post photographs of the Painted Desert for students to view. What colors do they see?

2. Set up work tables covered with plastic.

3. Mix one part glue to three parts water. Tear or cut colored tissue paper into squares, making pieces of varying sizes.

4. Select a combination of three colors to work with: blue, amethyst, and yellow, or rust, lilac, and red, to reflect the desert at sunrise or sunset.

5. Place one colored piece of tissue at a time onto art paper. Brush with glue and water mixture. Work each color in "earth layers," overlapping pieces to create different shades. Allow to dry.

6. Create a colorful bulletin board display titled *Our Painted Deserts.*

Optional Activity: Visit a local artisan who creates sand paintings. How is the design made? What tools does the artisan use to move colored sand from a top level to a lower level? Try making your own sand painting.

Desert Canyons

Information

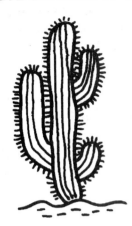

A canyon is a deep valley with steep sides. The word canyon comes from the Spanish *canon,* which means "hollow tube." Canyons are worn to great depths by the erosion of thousands of years and form some of the most spectacular scenery in the world.

The Grand Canyon is located in the Mojave Desert in Arizona. The walls of the Grand Canyon were formed over a period of millions of years by the Colorado River as it cut through layers of limestone, sandstone, shale, and gneiss. The layers vary in color and are especially brilliant at sunset. In some places the Grand Canyon is more than one mile (1.6 km) deep and between two to 18 miles (3 to 29 km) wide at the top. It is 217 miles (349 km) long!

The canyon of the Snake River in Oregon and Idaho averages 5,500 feet (1,680 meters) deep for 40 miles (64 km). Other beautiful canyons are found in Canada in the Rocky Mountains.

Project

Experiment to see how fast water sinks into the ground, drawing conclusions about how water relates to the formation of canyons.

Materials

- Small can with ends cut off
- Various types of soil
- Watch with a second hand
- Glass
- Water

Directions

1. Pour a full glass of water onto a soil surface. Use a watch to record the time at the start and at the time the water is no longer visible on the surface.

2. Set one end of the can firmly into the soil. Pour water to the top of the can. Clock the time it takes for the can to empty.

3. Repeat the same processes with different types of soil and compare the differences. What role do you think rain water played in the formation of the Grand Canyon?

19

Georgia O'Keeffe

Information

Georgia O'Keeffe was a famous American artist who settled in New Mexico in 1949. She found inspiration in nature for most of her paintings and her work reflected her great love of the North American deserts. She painted in a simple style with clear colors and sharp edges. Her flowers were painted very close up so that every detail and shade of color could be seen.

While living in New Mexico, O'Keeffe started to paint pictures of the bones of animals that had died in the Chihuahuan Desert. She liked the look of white bones against a bright blue sky. She loved to be out early in the wide open spaces with the sky towering above her. From these experiences she would create paintings of sunrises using only the primary colors—red, blue, and yellow.

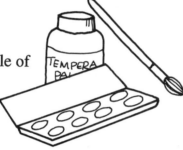

Project

Create a painting in the style of Georgia O'Keeffe.

Materials

- Tempera paints
- Watercolor paints
- Photographs of Georgia O'Keeffe's paintings
- Brushes
- Art paper

Desert Sunrise

Get up early one morning and study the early-morning sky, memorizing what you see. Using only red, blue, and yellow paint, create a painting of a sunrise.

Desert Flower

Pick a flower or buy one from a florist. Study it carefully, using a magnifying glass, if necessary. Use watercolors or watered-down tempera paint and paint one large flower. Include the tiniest details. Use light and dark shades of the same color.

Desert Bones

Gather some chicken or turkey bones. Wash and clean them thoroughly. Paint a picture of the bones against a blue sky.

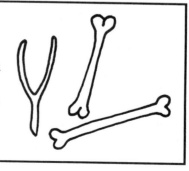

Kalahari Desert

Information

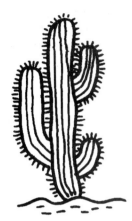

The Kalahari Gemsbok National Park was created in 1931 to protect *gemsboks* from poachers. This red sand desert park is 562 miles (904 km) from Johannesburg, South Africa, and is also home to other animals, but was named for the thousands of gemsbok that gallop there freely.

The Kalahari Desert in southern Africa is inhabited by several different kinds of antelopes—swift-moving animals with horns of varying shapes and sizes. Some of the most beautiful antelopes are the *oryxes*. The gemsbok is probably the most spectacular in the oryx family.

The gemsbok's face and legs and the underside of its body have distinctive streaks of black and white. The straight horns are about four feet (1.2 m) long and have pointed tips and ridged surfaces. These sharp horns are used as weapons when a gemsbok must defend itself against an enemy. If the animal is cornered and is unable to flee, it will lower its head and stab at the attacker with its deadly horns.

Project

- Write a description of the Kalahari Gemsbok National Park environment.
- Create a model to match the description.

Materials

- Internet access or reference books
- Sand, powdered red and brown tempera paint
- Clay
- Black and white paint
- Small trays for models

Directions

1. Connect to the Internet and choose the "Infoseek" search engine. Type in **gemsbok**. If you do not have internet access, use reference or travel books on Africa.

2. Click on *Kalahari Gemsbok National Park**. This red sand game park is on the border of Botswana in South Africa.

3. Based on the information found, write a description of the Kalahari's environment.

4 Create a three-dimensional model of the Kalahari. Mix powdered red and brown tempera paint with sand to make a reddish sand. Form gemsbok likenesses from clay, showing black and white streaks and horns. Add other features of the Kalahari Gemsbok National Park to match your written description.

*This website was current at time of publication.

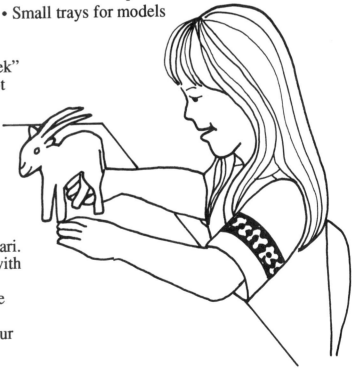

21

The Sahara Desert

Information

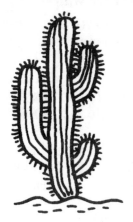

The Sahara Desert is the largest desert in the world and covers parts of ten countries. It is about 3.5 million square miles (9 million square km) in area, which is about the size of the U.S. The landscape of this vast African desert includes mountain ranges, rocky plateaus, gravelly plains, and huge seas of sand called *ergs*. The shifting sands of the ergs form sand dunes as high as 600 feet (183 meters). The rainfall averages less than eight inches (20 cm) per year.

Oases lie throughout the Sahara, with most of the water coming from wells or springs. There are about 90 large oases where people can live in villages nearby and grow crops such as dates, barley, and wheat. Some oases have thousands of date palm trees. Most of the Saharan people are *nomads* who tend herds of sheep, goats, camels, and cattle. They travel through the desert in search of water and grazing land.

Major deposits of oil and natural gas lie under the Sahara Desert in Algeria and Libya. These two countries are among the largest producers of these two sources of energy.

Project

- Plan a caravan.
- Taste dates.

Materials

- World Book (Sahara) and other resource books
- Large map of Africa
- Calculators
- Map scale
- Packaged dates (enough for one per student)

Directions

For this activity, students prepare to go on a caravan.

1. Use a large classroom map of Africa or enlarge the map of the Sahara Desert found in *World Book Encyclopedia*. Point out that the Sahara stretches across northern Africa from the Atlantic Ocean to the Red Sea and from the Atlas Mountains to the Sahel region covering parts of ten countries.

2. Divide class into groups of four or five students. Each group will work cooperatively to plan a caravan, using the Caravan Itinerary.

4. Use a map scale and a calculator to determine distances traveled.

5. Present your mapped route and completed itinerary to the class.

6. Taste dates for a culmination treat!

Caravan Itinerary

Caravans involve a great deal of planning. What will you need to pack? Which pack animals will you take? How many of each? Where will the caravan originate? What countries will you cross? How far will you travel? How long will it take? Work with your group to plan your caravan. Outline your route on the itinerary.

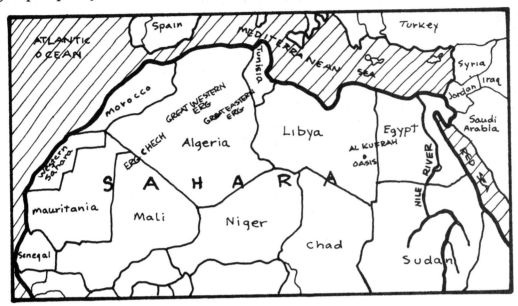

Where will you start? _____

What countries will you cross? _____

Name the mountains, ergs (vast sandy areas), oases, or rivers you will cross.

Mountains	Ergs	Oases	Rivers

Approximately how many miles or kilometers will you travel? _____

How many days will it take for your trip? _____

How many miles will your caravan average per day? _____

What pack animals will be part of the caravan? How many of each will you take?

___ Camels   ___ Mules   ___ Llamas   ___ Sheep

Deserts Activity Book

Cold Deserts

Information

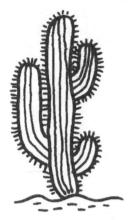

When most people think of deserts, regions with very high temperatures and sandy, dry land come to mind. But some of the world's deserts do not fit this description. These other deserts are called *cold deserts*.

The polar regions of the Arctic and Antarctic are considered cold deserts. As a result of the Earth's tilt, the sun shines in these regions for only part of the year. When it does, its rays slant through thick layers of the atmosphere. Temperatures are so low that very little frozen snow and ice melt. Very little rain falls. Because of the permanently low temperatures, water is always frozen and useless to living things. Such conditions make it hard for plants, animals, and people to survive.

The sea, however, supports a great deal of life. Algae grow in waters and are eaten by fish. The fish are food for seals which in turn are hunted by the polar bears. Birds, such as gulls, act as scavengers.

Project

Write a weather forecast and compare it to a forecast for a hot desert.

Materials

- Resource books
- Internet access
- Maps of polar regions

Directions

1. Use the Internet to get weather reports and weather forecasts for one of the polar regions. Do this for three or four days to see the temperature pattern. Print out the report each day. If access to the Internet is not available, use resource books to determine weather patterns and average temperatures of the polar regions.

2. With the information received, create a forecast for the following week. Include temperature highs and lows, wind patterns, snow forecasts, and special warnings.

3. Deliver your week's forecast as a TV weather person for a polar region.

4. Contrast the cold desert forecast with that of a hot desert such as the Sahara or the Kalahari.

Living in the Desert

Information

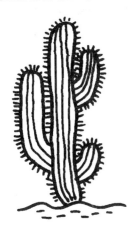

In spite of its harsh climate, the desert is able to support a large variety of plant life. The plants, in turn, make it possible for animals to exist in the desert. Like all living creatures, they depend upon green plants to supply the food they need. Where plants are plentiful in the desert, animals will be found as well—insects drink the nectar of desert flowers and spread the pollen, birds and small mammals eat the seeds of desert plants, and reptiles and larger mammals feed on the plant eaters.

Like the strong desert plants, the animals of the desert have developed various methods of surviving the harsh environment. The ability to cope well with the scarcity of water and to endure the heat and dryness of the desert is characteristic to animals that can live in the desert.

Project

Experiment to draw conclusions about sources of water for desert animals.

Materials

- A variety of juicy fruits
- Resource books on desert plants

Directions

1. Have a discussion about times when you were very thirsty: a hot summer day, at the beach, in a car, playing baseball or soccer. How did you satisfy your thirst?

2. What do people do at public parks, playgrounds, or in school where they might be thirsty and there are no water fountains? Brainstorm a variety of ideas (carry a thermos, buy a drink). Make a list of all responses.

3. Engage in an activity that makes you sweaty and thirsty. Before drinking any water, try eating samples of available fruits, including quartered apples, oranges, grapefruit, or slices of watermelon and other melons that may be available. Make notes about which fruits satisfied your thirst. Are any of these found in the desert?

4. Brainstorm a list of plant sources that would be available to desert animals that might help to provide water for them. Can you think of any other methods the animals have for meeting their water needs?

25

Desert Plants

Information

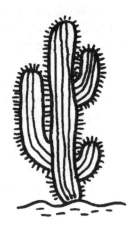

The list of plants that can survive and thrive in a desert environment is quite amazing. Trees, shrubs, grasses, weeds, and even flowers can live in the desert. But these plants are quite different from those that grow in areas with more moisture. They must be able to live with little water and endure extreme temperatures.

Plants compete for the precious water by spacing themselves far apart. In this way their roots have enough room to reach out and search for water. Some desert plants obtain water from deep beneath the earth. The mesquite (mes-KEET) tree has roots that extend as deep as 40 feet (12 meters). Cactus plants store large amounts of water in their leaves, roots, and stems.

Some plants survive by reducing the water loss which occurs through the leaves by shedding their leaves during a drought.

Project

Experiment to see how a cactus stores water.

Materials

- Sea sponge
- Shallow dish
- Water
- Measuring cup

Directions

When rain falls, a cactus soaks up water through its roots. Its tissues fill with water and the plant expands like an accordion. The stored water allows the cactus to survive for many months when there is no rain.

1. To get an idea of how a cactus stores water, pretend the sea sponge is a cactus plant. Pour water into a shallow dish to cover the bottom. Place the sponge in the center of the dish.

2. Observe what happens. After a few minutes, touch the sponge. How does it feel? Squeeze the sponge and let the water drip into the measuring cup. How much water did the sea sponge absorb?

3. Experiment with more water in a larger dish. Squeeze the sponge and measure the water a second time. Is more, less, or about the same amount of water released?

4. Experiment further with sea sponges of different sizes to simulate different-sized cacti. Draw conclusions about how much water is absorbed.

Yucca Plants

Information

Some desert plants are "water seekers." Their roots may extend as far as 100 feet (30 meters) below the ground to seek water. There, they may find underground streams and other sources of water. Or their roots may spread out in all directions to search for water.

The yucca grows abundantly in the southwestern part of the U.S. and in the highlands and plateaus of Mexico. Here, several species have become large and beautiful trees. The Joshua Tree National Monument in California contains important collections of yucca trees.

Native Americans have found many uses for this water-seeking plant. They make rope, sandals, mats, and baskets from the leaf fibers. They eat the buds and flowers either raw or boiled. The roots and stems are used for making soap. Yuccas also serve as decorative plants in gardens.

Project

Examine root systems of vegetables.

Materials

- A variety of fresh vegetables with taproots (a taproot is the enlarged part of a root that grows straight down)—carrots, beets, parsnips, radishes, turnips, and rutabagas

Directions

1. Set up a display of fresh vegetables with taproots. Observe and note the differences in the length of taproots. Which of the vegetables do you think can draw in the most water? Why?

2. Wash, slice, and serve carrots and radishes. Explain that children are actually eating the root of the vegetable.

3. Cook and sample other root vegetables.

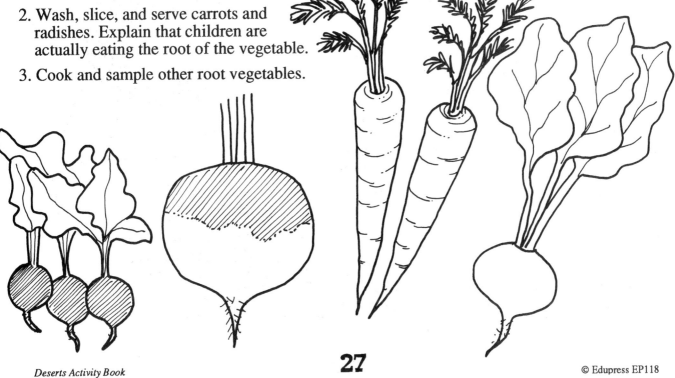

Cactus Plants

Information

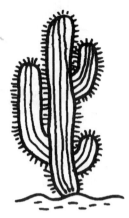

There are about 2,000 species of cactus plants. Most grow in hot, dry regions of Mexico and the southwestern part of the U.S., but some grow in rain forests and on mountains. Some even grow in Alaska and near Antarctica.

Most cactuses have thick, fleshy stems with waxy skin. The stem holds water, and the waxy skin keeps the water from evaporating. The surfaces of many cactuses can contract and expand to accommodate the amount of water being held. Cactuses have extremely long roots that grow close to the surface of the soil, enabling them to collect as much water as possible for storage.

The spines of a cactus plant protect it from being eaten by animals. Spines may be long or short, soft or sharp, and have straight or hooked tips. They grow in clusters out of small bumps called areoles. All cactuses produce flowers that also grow out of the areoles. The flowers are short-lived—some bloom for only a few days to help keep water from evaporating.

Project

Gather facts and have a class cactus conference.

Materials

- Cactus Conference page, following
- Resource books
- Paper bag

Directions

1. Make one copy of the following page. Cut out each cactus topic on the dotted lines. Fold each one in half and place all of them in a paper bag.

2. Each child reaches in, removes one topic, and writes his or her name on the paper.

3. Make a list of each topic and the student responsible for fact-finding. Set a time frame for each student to find three interesting facts about his or her topic.

4. For the cactus conference, invite children to sit in a circle. Each student tells what topic he or she is reporting on and presents the information found. Photographs may be used.

Cactus Conference

organ pipe cactus	barrel cactus
old man cactus	prickly pear cactus
jumping cholla cactus	saguaro cactus
spines of the cactus	cactus flowers
cactus seeds	growth of a cactus
importance of cactuses to birds	importance of cactuses to people
how a cactus stores water	ancient cactus plants
insects attracted to cactuses	different shapes of cactuses
protective features of cactuses	where cactuses grow
cactus stems	cactus roots
how cactuses protect birds and animals	pictures of different cactuses
how long cactuses may live	pollen and nectar of cactuses

Saguaro Cactus

Information

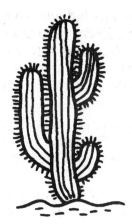

The saguaro cactus grows in the Sonoran desert which stretches through Arizona, California, and Mexico. The saguaro desert landscape appears still and statuesque with the 50-foot (15.24-m) tall cactus trees, but appearances can be deceptive. Saguaros can be full of activity. A number of different types of animals such as the Gila woodpecker, elf owl, and Harris hawk make their homes or nests in the prickly trunks and branches.

In May, when the saguaro cactus blossoms showing large milky-white flowers with yellow centers, bats, doves, and butterflies come to drink the nectar. As they do, they pick up and carry pollen to fertilize other flowers. The flowers and fruit of the saguaro feed many desert animals and insects as well as people. Without saguaros, there would be a great shortage of food and nesting places for many desert creatures.

This largest-of-all cactus plants can weigh up to several tons and live for 200 years, going through various phases in its interesting life cycle.

Project

Research the life cycle of the saguaro and create an illustrated time-line mural.

Directions

1. Read *Desert Giant* and *Cactus Hotel* to the class to give students illustrated, clear information about the life cycle of the saguaro cactus. (If these books are unavailable, use resource books to find the same information.)

2. Make a list of the phases of the saguaro's life cycle and what happens at each phase.

3. Divide into small groups of two to four students. Assign each group a phase in the saguaro's life cycle to research and illustrate. Mount the individual illustrations on the butcher paper to form a time-line of the life cycle.

4. Make a large saguaro out of green construction paper as a background for displaying the finished time line. Have children brainstorm ways to show prickly spines, either flat or three-dimensional.

Materials

- Butcher paper
- Watercolors, tempera paints, pastels, marking pens
- Green construction paper
- Scissors
- *Desert Giant* by Barbara Bash and *Cactus Hotel* by Brenda Z. Guiberson (see Literature List, page 3)
- Other resource books

Saguaro Seeds

Information

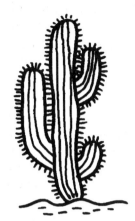

For centuries the Tohono O'odham (toh-HO-no o-O-dahm) Indians have enjoyed the harvest ritual associated with the saguaro cactus. Every June after the blossoms have dried, the seeds have ripened, and the fruit has formed, women and children go out into the desert to harvest the sweet fruit. Using long wooden poles, they reach up to pull the ripe fruit down from the cactus. The red pulp full of black seeds is scooped out and emptied into a bucket.

At a nearby location, the pulp is mixed with water and cooked for a long time until it is thick and sweet. Then it is strained to remove the seeds. From this saguaro fruit mixture, the Tohono O'odhams make jams and candies, wines, and syrups.

Back at the saguaro cactus trees, birds and ants enjoy the fallen pulp and seeds. Lizards sit quietly by waiting to make a meal of the ants! Coyotes enjoy leftovers in the evening.

Project

Make fresh fruit jam.

Directions

1. Take a class visit to a local farmer's market or to the produce section of your local supermarket to see what fruits are in season for making jam. Purchase fruit along with other ingredients needed in your recipe.

2. Cook fruit jam according to recipe instructions. Seeds may be left in or removed using a strainer or sieve. Decide which way you prefer the jam, or prepare two types for comparison.

3. Let mixture cool; pour into clean glass jars and refrigerate overnight.

4. Sample the jam in its pure form using small plastic spoons. Also serve on crackers.

Materials

- Fresh in-season fruit suitable for jams such as blueberries, strawberries, raspberries
- Pots, pans, wooden spoons for stirring
- A recipe for jam and listed ingredients
- Strainer or sieve
- Clean glass jars for canning
- Crackers
- Plastic spoons

Desert Flowers

Information

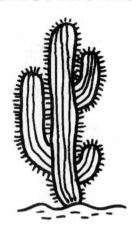

While cactus plants are "water storers" and other plants like the yucca and mesquite are "water seekers," some plants such as the Mexican goldpoppy are "drought evaders." This means that they are dormant during the long dry periods. They grow only after a heavy rainfall. The seeds may lie for a year or more in the desert soil without growing. A light rain is not strong enough to wash away the seeds' special coating, but a heavy rain will, allowing the seeds to grow.

Within a few weeks after a heavy rainfall, the seeds sprout, the plants grow quickly, and the flowers bloom. Blossoms of gold may carpet the desert in the spring. Other colorful flowers such as Arizona blue-eyes, blackfoot daisies, rain lilies, and angel trumpets cover the desert, too.

After the flowers bloom and scatter their seeds for the next year, they wither and die. The whole process takes only a few weeks.

Project

Create a pictorial calendar showing how desert flowers grow.

Directions

1. Duplicate the calendar page. Review the process of dormant seeds sprouting, growing, blossoming, scattering seeds, and dying.

2. Using two calendar pages, fill in the month name and the dates for two consecutive spring months.

   • Begin the cycle with a drawing of seeds lying dormant.

   • Select a date of heavy rainstorm and add an illustration.

   • Continue by showing the seeds sprouting and the subsequent stages of growth during the two-month period.

3. Mount the two pages side-by-side on construction paper. Make Mexican goldpoppies from yellow-orange crepe paper. Pinch the crepe paper together at the center to form a flower and glue to the construction paper to form a flower border.

Materials

• Calendar page, following
• Pencils
• Marking pens and colored pencils
• Three-inch (7.62-cm) squares of yellow-orange crepe paper
• Large piece of colored construction paper
• Glue

Sunday	Monday	Tuesday	Wednesday	Thursday	Friday	Saturday

33

Welwitschia

Information

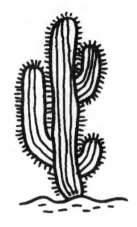

One of the most fascinating desert plants is Welwitschia (wehl -WHICH-ee- uh), a strange-looking plant found in the Namib Desert of southern Africa. This plant has long, strap-like leaves that can absorb dewdrops from the moisture of nighttime mists and fog.

The Welwitschia's short, woody trunk rises from a large taproot and spreads to a width of five to six feet (1.5 to 1.8 meters). It resembles a giant, flattened mushroom. A single pair of green leaves spills over the top. They are two to three feet (61 to 91 cm) wide and often twice as long. They are woody, grow from the base, and live as long as the plant does. The leaves are split into long, ribbonlike shreds by the hot desert winds.

Every year, stiff, jointed growths from six to 12 inches (15 to 30 cm) long develop where the leaves join the trunk. These growths bear small, erect flower spikes called cone clusters. Welwitschia plants live for 100 years or more.

Project

Visualize and draw a picture of the plant from a written description.

Materials

- Crayons and broad-tipped marking pens
- Drawing paper
- Reference book on desert plants or photograph of a Welwitschia

Directions

1. Write descriptive sentences of the Welwitschia plant on the chalkboard. Read the description orally to students, allowing them to visualize the plant as you describe it.

2. Distribute drawing paper, crayons, and markers. Ask students to create a drawing based on the written and oral description.

3. When all drawings are complete, compare drawings with photographs.

Deserts Activity Book

Desert Animals

Information

The desert is home to all types of animals—mammals, reptiles, birds, insects, and arachnids. Most animals avoid the heat of the desert sun during the day by feeding and hunting at night when the temperature has dropped. Most small animals survive by digging burrows and staying underground during the day. Larger animals try to find shady areas. Reptiles such as snakes and lizards have tough, leathery skin to protect them, but they look for shady areas too.

Desert animals must survive without much water. Rodents rarely drink. They get their water from the seeds and stems they eat. Birds get water from cactus fruit and other food. Snakes and lizards get their water from the animals they prey upon.

Most desert animals are nocturnal; they come out at night. Those that do move about during the day try to keep their bodies off the hot ground by hopping or running on tiptoe.

Project

Graph animals groups that live in the desert.

Materials

- Resource books
- Desert Life graph, following

Directions

1. Duplicate Desert Life graph.

2. Use resource books to create a list of mammals, birds, insects, and reptiles that live in the desert.

3. Transfer their list of desert animals to the graph, listing each in the appropriate category.

4. Using information from individual graphs, create a class graph. Discuss the following:
   - What category has the largest number of animals?
   - What category has the least?
   - What conclusions can you draw about why certain types of animals can live and survive in the desert climate?
   - What types of skin and protective features do these animals have?

Desert Animals

Mammals	Reptiles	Birds	Insects	Arachnids

Camels

Information

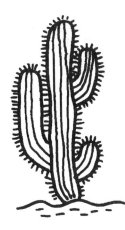

Of all the animals that live in the world's deserts, the camel is probably the best known. The *Arabian camel*, or *dromedary*, has a single hump. The two-humped *Bactrian camel* lives in the deserts of central Asia where winters are very cold and it grows a winter coat.

A camel's hump is used as a supply of food. The hump is mostly fat which can be used as a source of energy when other food is scarce. Camels can go for a long period of time without water because their bodies use small amounts of water very efficiently. The camel's temperature rises as the air gets hotter and drops when it gets cooler. This reduces the need to sweat and lessens the loss of water from its body.

Camels have fleshy pads on their feet that allow them to walk easily on soft sands where trucks would easily get stuck. They can carry people and heavy loads to places that have no roads. Because of these characteristics and the ability to survive well in the desert, camels are called "ships of the desert."

Project

Conduct an exercise to discover how difficult it may be for a camel loaded with cargo to stand up.

Materials

- Backpacks filled with different weights and loads
- Knee pads

Directions

Camels can drop to the ground and get up again—even with a heavy load on their back.

1. Put on knee pads to simulate tough, leathery pads that cover a camel's knees and act as cushions when it kneels. Drop to your knees and rest, then attempt to get up without using your hands.

2. Try a second time wearing a backpack loaded with books. Can you rise easily with added weight? Continue adding more weight until getting up becomes too difficult.

3. After everyone has had an opportunity to try this, have a classroom competition. Who can kneel and then rise with a loaded backpack the fastest?

Kangaroo Rats

Information

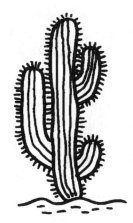

The kangaroo rat is a small rodent that belongs to the pocket mouse family. It has long and powerful hind legs and can jump around like a kangaroo. Its total length is only about 15 inches (38 cm), including its tail which is about eight inches (20 cm) long. Kangaroo rats have short front legs, large heads, and big eyes. Their silky fur is yellow or brown on the upper parts and white on the lower parts.

Kangaroo rats live in the deserts of the southwestern U.S. and Mexico. During the day they sleep and hide in burrows. At night they come out to gather plant food. They use their small front feet to stuff food into fur-lined pouches on the outside of their cheeks.

Then they carry their food back to their nests, careful to avoid kit foxes out hunting for them. To escape, the kangaroo rat jumps high, kicking sand in the fox's face, before running away.

Kangaroo rats do not need to drink water. They use the water that is produced in their bodies when food inside them combines with the oxygen they breathe.

Project

Create a day's diary of the habits and activities of the kangaroo rat.

Directions

As nocturnal creatures, kangaroo rats have very specific times of day when they sleep, gather food, and venture outside. They spend their days in the burrows they have dug where the air is moist and humid. This helps them survive and be comfortable.

1. Duplicate the journal page.

2. Use the Internet and other resources to find information about how a kangaroo rat lives.

3. Write a journal entry from the point-of-view of a kangaroo rat, describing the activities in your day and the time of day that these things are done. Be detailed in explaining why certain activities occur at specific times of the day.

4. Draw and color an illustration for your journal entry. Mount it with the journal page on construction paper for display.

Materials

- Internet access
- Resource materials
- Journal page, following
- Drawing paper
- Large sheet of construction paper
- Crayons or markers, pencil
- Glue

Kangaroo Rat Journal

_____

_____

_____

_____

_____

_____

_____

_____

_____

_____

_____

_____

_____

Deserts Activity Book

Kit Foxes

Information

As dusk descends on the deserts of North America, the kit fox begins to move quietly and swiftly through the shadows. No larger than a house cat, the kit fox is a skillful hunter preying on small rodents and insects that share its environment. The animal's large, fur-lined ears enable it to find its prey easily in the nighttime shadows. The kit fox's large ears move independently of each other so that it can listen for sounds coming from two different directions at the same time. Its hearing is very sharp—always alert to the slightest rustle of sand, rattle of twigs, or scurrying of feet in the quiet desert.

When a kit fox hears a sound indicating prey is close by, it scurries off to snatch a meal. Its sand-colored fur is good camouflage in the desert. The kit fox hunts only during the sunless hours. During the day, this small mammal finds shelter from the hot desert sun in its den—a long, narrow burrow dug deep in the cool soil beneath the desert floor.

Project

Experiment with sounds coming from two directions.

Materials

• An assortment of small rhythm instruments—triangle, wooden blocks, sticks, bells

Directions

1. Select two children to listen for sounds coming from different directions in the room. Select two children to make the sounds. "Listeners" should be facing away from the source of the sound so they can't see where it is coming from. "Sound-makers" should stand at opposite sides of the room.

2. Give an instrument to each "sound-maker." One "sound-maker" makes an instrument sound. The "listeners" indicate with their right or left hand which side of the room the sound came from. Vary the instruments. Give all children an opportunity to be a "listener" and a "sound-maker."

3. Increase the difficulty of listening by doing this activity in a space larger than a classroom. Is it harder to tell what direction a sound is coming from in a larger room? Add some background noise so "listeners" must fine-tune their listening skills. Vary the activity by trying different sounds and noises and having listeners wear ear muffs.

4. What conclusions can you draw about the ease or difficulty a kit fox has finding prey in the desert?

Desert Birds

Information

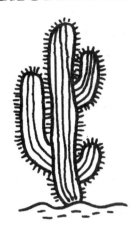

Few birds live in deserts because most birds are active during the day. Birds that eat seeds must drink every day, and most get their liquid by eating juicy insects. Desert birds must look hard to find their food. Some eat insects, some eat lizards, others eat cactus fruit.

Gila woodpeckers, elf owls, Harris hawks, and white-winged doves may make their nests in the tall saguaro cactus plant. This is a high, safe, and cool place where other desert animals cannot harm or eat the eggs. It is also a safe place for the birds. While feathers protect larger birds from the hot sun, small ones seek the shade of bushes and rocks.

The roadrunner is a long-legged desert bird that runs across the hot desert floor instead of flying through the cooler upper air. It relies on its legs and feet to catch prey or to escape from enemies, and is capable of running as fast as 15 miles (24 km) per hour. Roadrunners will eat just about anything—insects, mice, toads, snakes, lizards, cactus fruit. It can kill quick-moving desert reptiles by striking them with its large, hard beak.

Project

Experience eating like a desert bird in an eating race.

Materials

- Long covered table
- Food that can be eaten without utensils, hands, or assistance—watermelon slices work very well
- Paper plates and paper towels

Directions

1. Game rules are important for this activity. Groups of five or six children (or more) may race at the same time. No one may use hands or objects for assistance. Student is disqualified for doing so.

2. Set up long table with triangular slices of watermelon (or another easy-to-eat-with-the-mouth-only food). One student stands behind each slice. At a given signal, students race to finish the slice of watermelon—bending over and eating only with their mouth.

3. Student who finishes first in each group is the winner.

41

Desert Reptiles

Information

Lizards, snakes, and tortoises live in most deserts. They have tough, leathery skin with dry scales over their bodies. Reptiles do not sweat. Like desert mammals, they stay out of the hot sun and come out at night to hunt.

Reptiles are cold-blooded so their body temperature depends on their surroundings. When it is cool, they warm themselves in the sun. When it is hot, snakes and lizards keep cool by hiding in shady spots between and under rocks. Desert tortoises avoid the heat by burrowing into the ground. They scrape the soil with their strong legs and push it away with their shells.

Most lizards feed on insects and do not usually need to drink. Snakes prey on jerboas and kangaroo rats and get all the moisture they need from the blood of their prey. Like all desert animals, these reptiles must be able to live without much water. They get the liquid they need from the plants, insects, and animals they eat.

Project

- Make models to learn about the scaly skin of reptiles.
- Conduct an experiment to discover how rocks provide shelter in the desert.

Materials

- Self-hardening or oven-baked modeling clay
- Hard boiled-eggs
- Colored marking pens
- Plastic sheet

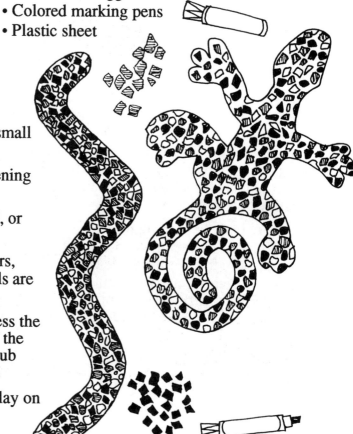

Directions

1. Set up a plastic-covered work table. Work in small groups.

2. Follow package directions to soften self-hardening or oven-baked modeling clay in your hands.

3. Mold the clay into the shape of a snake, lizard, or tortoise.

4. Color hard-boiled eggs with felt-tipped markers, using a variety of colors and making sure shells are completely colored.

5. Peel and break the shells into small pieces. Press the pieces of colored eggshell all over the body of the reptile. To make the eggshells adhere firmly, rub water into the clay as each piece is pressed on.

6. Allow reptiles to dry and set thoroughly. Display on a table with sand.

Desert Reptiles

Desert rocks absorb the sun's heat. This provides desert animals a cool refuge as they seek shelter from the desert's heat. Conduct an experiment in order to understand how rocks can provide a cool shelter, even as they are exposed to the sun.

Materials

- A variety of different-sized rocks
- Desert resource books or photographs

Directions

1. Collect a variety of different-sized rocks.

2. Pile them igloo-style in several small piles of varying size. Be sure that all of the piles are in the hot sun.

3. Feel the rock piles after a few hours. Touch the rocks on top. Touch the rocks on the bottom which are in a shaded area covered by the top rocks. Are the shady rocks at the bottom cooler than the rocks on top?

4. Look at photographs of rocky areas in the desert. Point out some places that would make suitable shelters for desert animals.

5. Use the rocks to build one large sun shelter and conduct the experiment again. Is the temperature of the rocks at the bottom of the large shelter different than that in the small sun shelters? Draw conclusions about your findings.

Rattlesnakes

Information

Several different kinds of rattlesnakes live in the North American deserts. One of the most interesting of these poisonous snakes is the sidewinder, so named because it has an unusual method of moving—or locomotion. It sidewinds its way across the loose sand of the desert floor. When it crawls, it moves its body in a series of sideways curves that leave J-shaped tracks in the sand. Sidewinding is an efficient way to move over loose sand, and several African snakes move in this same way.

Sidewinders of the North American deserts do their sidewinding only during the cool night hours. During the day they rest quietly in the shade or buried in the sand. At night, the snakes come to life and slither through the shadows searching for rodents, lizards, and other small animals for their dinner. The sidewinder finds its prey using a small sense organ on its head that reacts to heat put out by other animals' bodies. When the sidewinder locates its prey, it bites with its hollow fangs that inject venom. Its victim dies quickly.

Project

Move like a sidewinder.

Directions

Remind children a day before this activity to wear play clothes to school.

1. View a video of sidewinder rattlesnakes if available.

2. Take the class to a large open indoor area in the school. Have two to three children at a time attempt to sidewind across the room. Hands must remain still and cannot be used to aid movement.

3. When all of the children have had a turn, ask for volunteers to have a sidewinder race. Allow four to five students to race against each other.

Materials

• A large, open indoor area, preferably one with smooth floors to slide on
• Play clothes
• Video of rattlesnakes, if available

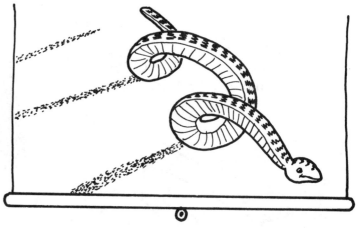

Insects and Arachnids

Information

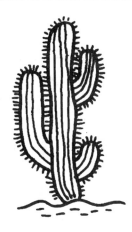

Many types of insects are found in deserts and some are very important to the life cycle of plants. Bees and flies sip the nectar from the flowers of cactus plants and then spread the pollen to fertilize other plants.

Flies, wasps, ants, and termites live underground and do well in deserts, but the most successful insects are the desert beetles. Some insects only come out at night, while others are active in the hottest part of the day. Ants and termites eat trees and plants. Then they become food for lizards and other insect-eating desert animals.

Spiders of all sizes live in the desert. The largest is the tarantula. Camel spiders feed on insects and scorpions. Scorpions are usually yellow and live under rocks or stones. They also dig burrows with their claws. Scorpions use the poison in the tip of their tail to kill their insect prey. They do not drink often but make do with the blood of their victims.

Project

Identify insects and arachnids that live in the desert.

Directions

1. Duplicate the spider web page.

2. Using reference materials, create a list of insects and arachnids that live in the desert.

3. Draw pictures of at least six of the insects and arachnids on your list. Color and cut out. Glue them to the spider web.

Materials

- References on insects and arachnids
- Spider web page, following
- Paper
- Pencil
- Markers or crayons
- Scissors
- Glue

Deserts Activity Book   © Edupress EP118

Insects and Arachnids

Glossary Game

You've spent quite a bit of time in the desert. See if you know what these words mean. Draw a line to connect each word to its definition.

irrigate

valley

canyon

dunes

erosion

arroyo

mesquite

saguaro

cactus

nomads

desertification

caravan

oasis

reptile

a long train of people and pack animals that travel across the desert

a small desert tree with deep roots

a large cut in the land made by rivers

people who move from one place to another as a way of earning a living or in search of water and grazing land

low land between hills or mountains

the wearing away of land and rock by wind, water, rain and other forces of nature

a spiny, prickly, mostly leafless plant able to store water and survive desert climate

to supply the land with water using pipes and ditches

a cold-blooded animal whose skin is covered with scales

a fertile area in the desert near a spring or underground stream

the largest cactus plant that can grow up to 50 feet (15.24 m) and live up to 200 years

a process by which land becomes unable to support plant or animal life

a cut in the land made by rushing rainwater

mounds of sand created and shaped by the wind

Score: If you got all 14 correct, you're real HOT—like the desert!
If you got 11-12 correct, you're very warm!
If you got 10 or fewer correct, you need to come out of your burrow!

47

World Wide Web

Are you ready to do some more desert exploring? There's plenty of information on the World Wide Web. The web pages below were active at publication date but their continued presence is not guaranteed. Animals, plants, desert lore, and exploration ideas are all there waiting for you.

Address	Content
www.desertusa.com/life.html	*Desert Life in the American Southwest* —information on all the U.S. deserts, including tours of wildlife and plant life.
www.cuug.ab.ca.8001/~animal/deserts.html	*Animalwatch-Deserts*—a link from the Animalwatch home page, find basic desert facts and pictures of desert animals.
library.advanced.org/11353/text/desert.htm	*Save Our Earth and Make a Difference* —an exploration of the desert biome and a description of how and why the world's deserts are expanding.
www.amnh.org/science/expedition/index_map.html	*An Expedition to the Gobi Desert*— information about the American Museum of Natural History's 1990 expedition.
www.azstarnet.com/~sasi/	*Sonoran Arthropod Studies Institute*— learn about desert arthropods and take a virtual tour of the Sonoran Desert.